GRANDMOTHER MOON SPEAKS

Simon Otto
Illustrated by James McCann

Thunder Bay Press

Lansing, Michigan

Published by Thunder Bay Press/Sam Speigel
Designed and typset by Maureen MacLaughlin-Morris
Illustrated by James McCann
Printed by Baker Johnson, Inc., Dexter, Michigan
Cover painting by James McCann

ISBN: 1-882376-10-2

Printed in the United States of America

03 04 05 06 07   2 3 4 5 6 7 8 9

Lansing, Michigan

TABLE OF CONTENTS

Introduction 2

How It Is 4

CREATION OF MAN 7

Sharing Ways of Our People 11

Grandfather's Wisdom 14

THE RACE 17

Our Animal Brothers 20

Bi-Culture: Good or Bad? 22

MOTHER EARTH HAS ANSWERS 25

Progress 28

Home Life 30

THE THREE LIVES 33

Coming of Age 37

Pow-Wow 41

SWEET DISCOVERY 45

The Burnout 48

Indian Veterans of the Civil War 51

A CHANGE OF SEASON 55

Happenings of Mother Earth 57

Names of Months 59

TALE OF THE TAMARACK 63

Mother Earth's Messengers 66

BIRTH OF FOG 69

Indian Spiritual World 71

THE FIRST BEAVER 75

A Visit With The Animal Brothers 77

BROTHER SKUNK'S PUNISHMENT 81

The Old Village 84

REBIRTH 89

The Raid 91

THE COMING OF WINTER 95

Northern Lights and Why 97

Glossary 99

INTRODUCTION

I am of Indian heritage, my father being Chippewa (*Ojibway*), and my mother being Ottawa (*Odawa*). I was born and raised in northern Michigan where there was a fairly large Indian population. I was one of ten children, three boys and seven girls; a large family by any standards. The house was ruled and run by my mother.

My father and mother were very interested in the preservation of their culture and practiced it most of the time. My grandfather lived with us and he was also instrumental in the dissemination of the Indian ways. Across the road lived *Seeson* (Susan), an Indian woman steeped in herbal knowledge of plants. All these people were instrumental in my upbringing. Their stories and happenings made an impact on my everyday life.

Many visitors came to our house and I often sat and listened to them. They talked in the Indian language most of the time, interspersing their conversation with English. Because I understood some Indian words, I could follow most of the conversation.

The reason I couldn't talk in the Indian language was because of my mother. When she was a young girl, she attended a government-run Indian school. At the age of eight, she couldn't speak or understand English, but she was punished for speaking her native tongue. She vowed that when she married and had children, they would not learn the Indian language.

My father wanted to help preserve what was left of our culture and tradition. Many people came to our house for meetings: Andrew Wasaquam, John Ance,

Huron Petoskey, Gene Marks, Frank Michigan, Fred Ettawageshik, and many others whose names I don't remember. In later years, there were Sam Shenonquat, Susie Shagonaby, Harrison Blake, and Isaac Naska.

They talked of things pertaining to the area Indians. Because it is customary to share with others the wonders of your culture they also told stories. I was allowed to stay and listen, but I had to be quiet. The sing-song sound of the language and the stories fascinated me. Some tales sounded strange but, as I was to learn later in life, the Indian world I grew up in was real.

Stories and legends from the Indian world are often similiar but they are not told the same. They differ in interpretation among the more than 300 tribes of America. The storyteller will tell the story as it was told to him, so there are many different versions. For instance, many stories mention *Nana-boo-shoo*. *Nana-boo-shoo* can change into many different forms, both animal and human. He is a close friend of the Great Spirit and the Indian people sought out his advice or met with him for consultation. Stories about *Nana-boo-shoo* can be different in locations as little as ten miles apart. I have listened to many different storytellers, and their words and wisdom are a gift from the Great Spirit.

4

HOW IT IS

Perhaps I'd better take time to explain some words that will appear often in these writings. They are familiar to me, but I know better when my wife says, "What's that mean?"

Most Indian tribes have their own way of pronouncing certain words. If it is not the way your family says them, please respectfully bear with me. For those who have no idea what a word means, the following explanations will be helpful. Some words I will be using often are:

Nana-boo-shoo. He can take on animal, human, or other forms. His role is like that of a magician: he can be a trickster. This may sound far-fetched, but in the Indian world it is not questioned. It is a belief handed down from generation to generation. By way of comparison, the Irish have the "little people" and the Norwegians, the "trolls." I respect the beliefs of every culture. The stories we hear stick in our minds and are part of what we refer to as our "roots."

"Mu-kaw-gee" (Dog). The faithful friend and companion of *Nana-boo-shoo*. In many Indian stories, animals can talk because the stories take place before mankind was on Mother Earth. Both *Mu-kaw-gee* and *Nana-boo-shoo* appear regularly in Indian stories.

My writings are divided into two categories: stories and "happenings." All of them I've heard from the Elders (Wise Ones). The Elders have lived long and have experienced life to the fullest. But one must be patient because Elders only speak when they trust. It's not in our culture to ask questions directly. Elders deserve respect and it must be shown. I, too, am an Elder, but I still revere those older than myself, who have much knowledge and speak with a voice that is smooth, soft, and knowing. Until next time, may you

Walk in Peace.

CREATION OF MAN

Since the genesis of time, each culture has recorded their version of the creation of man. Some of these theories place the beginning of man in different parts of the world. Each culture would like their version to be the basis of creation. Likewise, the Indians had their own stories about creation.

My Grandfather was a lumberman and trapper by trade and a member of the *Odawa* (Ottawa) tribe from the Grand River Band in the southwestern part of Michigan. He roamed Michigan in his early childhood, entering and leaving Canada at will. Through association with many *Ojibways* (Chippewas), he picked up stories and legends around the campfires. The following he related to me when I was a small boy.

Each tribe or band of Indians has its own version of the Creator. He is called the Great Spirit, *Manitou*, or Great One. The Creator in this story is called *Nana-boo-shoo*.

In the first stage of creation, *Nana-boo-shoo* created Mother Earth and put upon it woods, lakes, hills, mountains, and different animals. After all that work he was very tired. Now *Nana-boo-shoo* was a special kind of creator; he wanted someone he could talk to and so all the animals could speak. Although *Nana-boo-shoo* had a favorite animal, *Mu-kaw-gee* (Dog), with whom he talked, he was still dissatisfied.

One day, while *Nana-boo-shoo* and *Mu-kaw-gee* were lying on the south side of a hill dozing, *Nana-boo-shoo* said to *Mu-kaw-gee*, "I wish you had a body like mine, eyes to see what I can see, a mouth to taste, and a mind to create things like I do."

Mu-kaw-gee looked at *Nana-boo-shoo* and thought, *I feel good just the way I am. I am happy, I have plenty to eat and a good friend to talk to. Why is he not satisfied with this and all the other animals of the forest?*

Mu-kaw-gee said, "*Nana-boo-shoo*, I have a great idea! Since you have created Mother Earth, tree, hills, lakes, rivers, and all the animals, why don't you make someone like yourself? Then you will have someone with whom to talk."

Nana-boo-shoo said happily, "That's a good idea! But I want this to be part of Mother Earth." As they sat on the side of the hill thinking deeply on what to do and how, *Nana-boo-shoo* looked down the hill and saw a small creek.

He told *Mu-kaw-gee*, "Go down to the creek and get me some clay." *Mu-kaw-gee*, happy because he was helping *Nana-boo-shoo*, ran down to the creek, got a big mouthful of clay, and brought it back.

Together they built an oven, gathered some wood, and built a huge fire. *Nana-boo-shoo* took the clay and fashioned it into an image like himself, put it in the oven, and stoked the fire.

Then *Nana-boo-shoo* and *Mu-kaw-gee* lay down on the hillside and let the sunshine warm their bodies. As the sun beat down on them they began to get sleepy and soon they were both asleep.

After a while *Mu-kaw-gee* woke up, and shaking *Nana-boo-shoo* said, "I think it's done." *Nana-boo-shoo* went to the oven and took out the image of himself.

But he was disappointed. The fire had been too hot and the image was too dark. He thought, *What should I do with it? I know, I'll put it on the other side of the big water.* He placed it in what is now Africa.

Nana-boo-shoo told *Mu-kaw-gee*, "Our fire was too hot, we'll try again."

Wood was collected and fire was again lit. *Mu-kaw-gee* went to the creek and got another mouthful of clay and *Nana-boo-shoo* fashioned another image, put it in the oven, and stoked the fire. Again *Nana-boo-shoo* and *Mu-kaw-gee* lay down in the sunshine. This time *Nana-boo-shoo* told *Mu-kaw-gee*, "We won't sleep that long."

They slept, but this time it was only a short nap. Upon waking they ran to the oven and took out the image. But it was too soon and it was too light. *Nana-boo-shoo* thought about the dark man he had put in Africa and decided, *I'll put this one someplace else.* He reached across the big water and put it in what is now called Europe.

Now *Nana-boo-shoo* was determined. He told *Mu-kaw-gee*, "The first time we made it too hot. The man turned black. The second time we took it out too soon, and it was too light. So now we must not sleep, but tend the oven."

Again, *Nana-boo-shoo* sent *Mu-kaw-gee* to the creek for more clay. *Nana-boo-shoo* fashioned another image, collected wood, and built the fire just right. He put the image into the oven, but this time they sat near the oven door and looked in from time to time. They kept the fire going just right. Everything was going just fine.

Then *Nana-boo-shoo* looked into the oven and a smile came over his face. He called *Mu-kaw-gee*. "Its done," he said happily. Tenderly, he took the image out of the oven; it was a light brown.

"Beautiful!" he said, "I shall leave it right here in America."

Thus the American Indian was created.

Walk in Peace

SHARING WAYS OF OUR PEOPLE

In the world of the Indian, there is a real closeness of sharing. Most young people are not aware of this. Two sharing situations concern praise and shame. When an Indian does something good, the whole group shares in the praise that is merited by his good action. On the other hand, if he does something bad or shameful, the whole group suffers the blame with him. He brings the whole group shame by his bad behavior.

In the days of old when an Indian performed a brave deed, he didn't do it just for himself. He did it for the village, and the whole village profited by it. Tribes were strong because of brave deeds performed by the men. Thus other bands joined in, to ensure stronger unified tribes.

Little is written about Indians who became chiefs due to their acts of bravery and cunning; only a few books tell the stories of Sitting Bull, Pontiac, Chief Joseph, and many others. These chiefs were gifted with the talents of leadership and planning. They were generals of armies in their own right, were sought for advice, and were respected for being knowledgeable of strategy.

In the non-Indian system when some people did outstanding things, they did it for themselves and for their own personal glory. The Indian did outstanding things, not for his personal glory, but for all his people.

Indian people have a sense of togetherness, of being Indian, together. So when he does something good, all Indians share in his good deed. Most Indians will say, "He's Indian," and be pleased for him. Then he becomes even prouder of himself because he is an Indian. He, in turn, shares in the good deeds and honor of another Indian and the whole group or village gains esteem.

But this concept can also work the other way. When an Indian misbehaves, the whole group or village is made ashamed. When this happens, derogatory remarks are made about the village or group. But, of course, the whole group or band should not be condemned for the sins of a few.

Sometimes, when an Indian begins to participate by serving on committees or boards, the other Indians will get jealous of him and will begin to talk about him in a negative way. This is wrong. Every time an Indian dares to grow or raises his head above the crowd, other Indians should be proud and give him a boost or a pat on the back. They should remember the value of sharing and generosity. When a person of the village rises, he is taking the whole group up with him. They share in his honor.

In the days of old the village or group never was jealous and they never talked about one another. They were glad for the person, because they were sharing in and profiting by his honor and good deeds.

The Indian value of sharing and generosity refers not only to sharing food and shelter. It also includes the sharing of praise and shame.

Walk in peace

GRANDFATHER'S WISDOM

I have visited the land of my brothers, the *Winnebagos*, *Oneidas*, and *Ojibways* in the state of Wisconsin. I saw the pictured rocks where my great-great-grandmother and her parents canoed the great lake of Superior. They were of the wandering tribes. Now I recognize in myself the inheritance of "restless and itchy feet."

Upon my return home, I looked around and noticed the many things to be done. The grass had grown tall. In my neighborhood yards and lawns are well-kept, so I decided I must cut the grass. The first obstacle was that the lawnmower, a one-cylinder monster, wouldn't start. Apparently the water and dampness had taken their toll. However, after a few choice words from me it started and I followed obediently behind.

As I was cutting the grass, I wrestled in my mind with many mixed emotions about cultural values and modern living. But in the end "keeping up with the Joneses," the dominant life-style in society today, won out. Wearing my moccasins and a tee-shirt with my Indian name on it (made for me by my daughter), I cut the grass.

While doing so, pictures of my early childhood suddenly flashed through my mind. I remembered the time while, on my way to the Blackrobe's School, I noticed some well-kept lawns. I wondered what our little patch of lawn would look like if it was properly cut. That afternoon on the way home from school, I stopped at a neighbor's house and borrowed his lawnmower. I took it home and started to cut the grass.

Suddenly, a torrent of French words, mixed with Indian, poured down on me. It was as though I had committed the worst sin on earth! My Grandfather told me, "You don't cut the hair of Mother Earth to make it look good. The Great Spirit created the animals of the woods and birds of the waters to keep the grass short."

I suddenly realized that was why we had a big flock of geese. They kept the grass clipped short because it was their natural food. They were also good watch dogs, letting you know when someone or something was around. And they provided food for us later on.

Again, I bowed to Grandfather's wisdom.

Walk in Peace

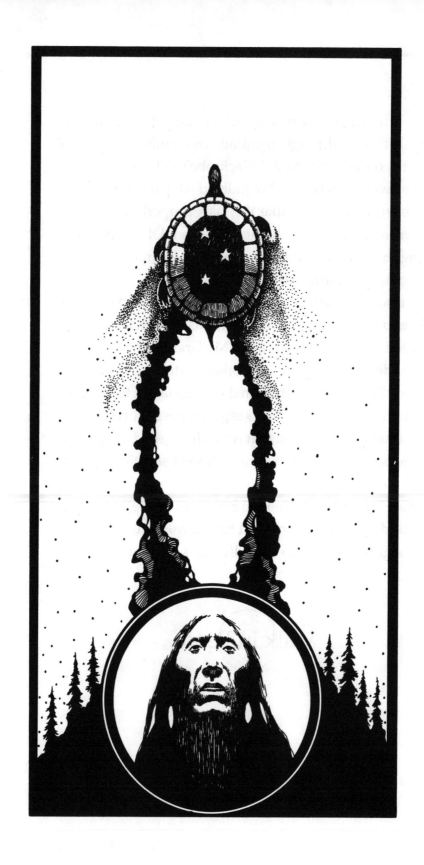

James M McCann 94
Ottawa

THE RACE

It was one of those warm days when *Nana-boo-shoo* was lying on his favorite hillside soaking up the warmth of Brother Sun. Suddenly his rest was interrupted by loud voices. He rolled over and tried to ignore them, but the voices kept getting louder. Angrily, he rose and headed toward the voices which were coming from near the lake.

As *Nana-boo-shoo* approached the source of the voices, he recognized *She-ke* (Mud Turtle) and his cousin, *O-doon-she-ke* (Snapping Turtle). Each was saying he could swim faster than the other. They asked *Nana-boo-shoo* to judge their swimming contest. But *Nana-boo-shoo* was in a bad mood. He told them that he could swim faster than either of them.

The turtles laughed at him, "What? *Nana-boo-shoo*? Faster than us?"

Nana-boo-shoo said angrily, "Okay! Let's race across the lake. First one on the other side is the winner, and the loser has to prepare dinner for the others."

The turtles talked it over and decided it was a fair challenge. So they told *Nana-boo-shoo*, "Come, let's go to the big lake for the race."

Secretly they thought they had the upper hand over *Nana-boo-shoo*. The lake was deep and cold and was many miles across. It was said that the lake was so wide that it took a brave five suns to get to the other side. The turtle's plan was this: because *Nana-boo-shoo* was sure to follow them they would immediately go to the bottom of the lake where it was cold and dark. They were accustomed to it, but *Nana-boo-shoo* was not.

The race was on. As they approached the water, *Nana-boo-shoo* told the turtles to go ahead because they were smaller and getting through the surf and rough waters would be hard for them. But to his surprise, they took advantage of the undertow and were soon out into deep water.

Nana-boo-shoo started swimming. He looked for the turtles on the surface of the lake but he couldn't see them anywhere. Then he looked down towards the bottom of the lake where he saw the turtles swimming furiously. *Nana-boo-shoo* started swimming faster.

The turtles looked up and saw *Nana-boo-shoo* and said to each other, "Well, he caught up with us. We'll swim faster."

But no matter how fast they swam, *Nana-boo-shoo* kept up with them. Soon *O-doon-she-ke* tired. He was not used to such a long swim in such cold water and he dropped out.

Nana-boo-shoo saw him drop out and chuckled, "One down, one to go."

She-ke was mad that *O-doon-she-ke* had left him to finish the race. Now it was up to him to show *Nana-boo-shoo* that he was the faster swimmer. An idea came to *She-ke*. "I'll go deeper where *Nana-boo-shoo* can't see me." Down he went.

Soon *Nana-boo-shoo* decided that he would go down to where *She-ke* was. Down *he* went. He could see *She-ke* swimming way ahead of him. *Nana-boo-shoo* swam faster.

She-ke, seeing *Nana-boo-shoo* gaining on him, got another idea. "I'll run on the bottom and stir up the mud. It will get in his eyes, and he won't be able to see." Down he went. *Nana-boo-shoo* followed.

She-ke smiled, "He's following my plan, it won't be long now and he'll drop out."

But *Nana-boo-shoo* realized what *She-ke* was doing and decided to swim just above him so he could follow the muddy trail.

She-ke and *Nana-boo-shoo* swam faster and faster. Suddenly they came to a sheer underwater cliff. *She-ke* turned quickly and headed straight up, swimming fast and furious. *Nana-boo-shoo* was close behind. As *She-ke* headed up he began to look for the light from Brother Sun, but he couldn't see it.

She-ke looked back and saw *Nana-boo-shoo* close behind him. He swam faster and then even faster! Suddenly *She-ke* came out of the water and shot straight up into the sky with *Nana-boo-shoo* close behind him. *She-ke* swam through a huge cluster of stars thinking to lose *Nana-boo-shoo* in them. But *Nana-boo-shoo* kept coming.

As they swam across the heavens, a collection of stars formed in their wake. Thus the Milky Way was formed because of a race between *She-ke* and *Nana-boo-shoo* that took place long ago in the "big lake."

Walk in Peace

OUR ANIMAL BROTHERS

Among the many walks of life are the conservationists, ecologists, and animal lovers. By nature and inheritance, I fall among those categories.

Whether the day is dark and dreary, or the sun is shining brightly, life goes on, and I accept it. There isn't much you can do about the weather. Today is a dreary day, but the sun is shining above the clouds and it is great to be alive and well. We have much for which to be thankful.

Our bird feeder is busy and much can be learned from the occupants. One of my favorite birds is the *Miska-bine-she* (Cardinal). I have seen them come and go to the feeder for quite some time now. They are beautiful birds; the male plumage a bright red, with a feathered crest, and the female a muted red. Their life style is to set up territorial rights and I imagine their song signals all other cardinals to keep their distance.

Lately, the female cardinal has been feeding in the morning and again in the evening. She must have a nest somewhere nearby, but probably she has no little ones or else she would be carrying seeds. I have observed the behavior and feeding pattern of the two

adults. Usually the two of them come together. The female will sit back from the feeder and the male will go to the feeder, get a few seeds and take them to the female. What dedication, love and sharing they have together!

But there is a sad note. *Ad-jid-ah-moo* (Red Squirrel), who has been visiting our feeder on a daily basis, has met his end. He had been hit by *Da-bon* (Car), probably by one who cares not for wildlife and sped up to scare the squirrel. He had to cross the road from his favorite tree, *Aw-nib* (Elm), to feed. It is but one more facet in the balance of nature that the Great Spirit had deemed necessary. It may seem cruel, but it is necessary. Had it not been a car, *Ad-jid-ah-moo* could have been killed by hawks or an owl. Even though *Ad-jid-ah-moo* frustrated me at times because he would gorge himself and chase the birds away from the feeder, I still feel sad. He was a neighbor and a visitor to our house. Life in *Aw-nib* goes on and there are still a lot of other squirrels running around. They have adjusted to his absence, much as people do.

Another day is ending. Death and devotion alike are observed in the lives of our wild brothers–but they persevere, in spite of the odds. They give me strength by their example.

Walk in peace

BI-CULTURE
GOOD OR BAD?

As Native Americans our heritage can be traced back thousands of years. We have endured nearly 500 years of overlordship by alien cultures. However, despite the obstacles that confront us our traditions endure.

A young Indian, in his pre-school years, lives in a totally different culture. School is an outside, alien world. He must change or keep his fears and feelings to himself. Usually, he chooses the latter until he is safely at home where he is comfortable. Humble though it may be, he knows how to exist and cope in that environment.

His family may be low-income. Housing is probably rented and is sub-standard, often owned by the government. If an Indian owns his own home, he may have no funds to make improvements. Thus, today's Indian youth must accept this way of life and make the best of it.

By the time an Indian youth reaches adolescence, the traditions and culture of the Indian community have been instilled in him. During the day he copes with the white world at school, but at night he retreats into the Indian community to be influenced and swallowed up by peer groups.

Slowly he comes to the realize that he does not fit into the mainstream. Assimilation is very hard for him: too much alienation, too little motivation, and self-esteem become an illness. He suffers an identity problem: how can he be an Indian in a dominant white society? The mainstream passes him by and he makes no attempt to join. How can he be expected to surmount these forces? Perhaps too little has been done for him to help him understand the non-Indian world and its ways. Assistance in housing, education, and rights is fine, but what about his psychological well-being?

Growing up today is difficult for anyone, but living in a bi-cultural world is an additional challenge. The security of home, the closeness of family, friends and peers–all have a great effect on one's lifestyle and mind. To be Indian in a non-Indian world is not easy. Stereotyping, prejudice, racism, bigotry, and exploitation are everyday occurrences in some Indian lives. Coping with and handling them varies with the individual. To be Indian in the Indian world is great. To be Indian in a dominant white society is a psychological challenge.

Walk in Peace

MOTHER EARTH HAS ANSWERS

During the early days of Mother Earth, all animal life was compatible, no hardships or displeasures were known, and man and animal cooperated. They strove to work with one another so they would be in accordance with the wishes of the Great Spirit.

Nish-na-be (First Man) and *Nish-na-be-quay* (First Woman) were living in harmony with one another and children came along as the Great Spirit said they would. Man enjoyed a bliss indescribable to us. All was perfect on Mother Earth in its early stages.

Among the animals was *Mu-kaw-gee* (Dog). He was a friend of the Indian and their conversations were happy and of mutual interest because they were both rearing families. But *Mu-kaw-gee's* life was somewhat different from the life of *Nish-na-be*. *Mu-kaw-gee's* off-spring came in litters of five to seven. At first *Mu-kaw-gee* accepted his big family but, later on when the third and fourth litters came along and the first litter was reproducing too, it began to be a problem.

Mu-kaw-gee had to look for more living room. *Nish-na-be* told him that he could help him put up a bigger shelter. So *Mu-kaw-gee* gathered his clan and they worked side by side with his friend *Nish-na-be*. They were fathers and providers and they had much to talk about. This made them even closer.

Later when even more children were born to both of them they began to think seriously about housing and food. They talked about their mutual problems, but they found no answers. *Mu-kaw-gee* and *Nish-na-be* said, "Let's talk to *Nana-boo-shoo* because he's wise and will be able to help us."

So off to *Nana-boo-shoo's* hill they went. The found him soaking up Brother Sun's warmth and enjoying the gentle, warm breezes of *Shaw-wah-nong* (South Wind). He opened one eye and saw *Nish-na-be* and *Mu-kaw-gee* coming. He grumbled a little because they were disturbing his nap. But then he then noticed that *Mu-kaw-gee* and *Nish-na-be* were not smiling and they looked very serious. Most of the time the two of laughed and talked as noisily as the pesky red squirrel.

After *Nana-boo-shoo* greeted *Mu-kaw-gee* and *Nish-na-be*, he offered them some food and asked what he could do for them. *Mu-kaw-gee* and *Nish-na-be* told him their stories: their families had grown so large that it had become difficult to find housing and to produce enough food for them to eat.

Nana-boo-shoo told them, "Let me think about it. Come back tomorrow. I should have an answer for you then." *Nana-boo-shoo*, not sure what he could tell them, thought: *I guess I had better talk to the Great Spirit.*

So he set out for the highest hill in the area because that's where the Great Spirit was usually found. As he approached the hill, he mulled over what he would say. When he reached the top of the hill, he burned his medicine and called out, "Oh Great Spirit, hear what *Nana-boo-shoo* has to say." Then he told everything as *Nish-na-be* and *Mu-kaw-gee* had told him. He waited.

Then suddenly the Great Spirit said, "Do not worry. I'll take care of it. Tell *Nish-na-be* and *Mu-kaw-gee* they'll have to look for a sign, but to be sure to be packed and ready to move."

So next day when *Nish-na-be* and *Mu-kaw-gee* returned, *Nana-boo-shoo* told them what the Great Spirit had said. *Nana-boo-shoo* told them to be patient, that the Great Spirit would give them a sign. So *Mu-kaw-gee* and *Nish-na-be* went home and told everyone to pack up their belongings because they would be going someplace, sometime, somehow.

The Great Spirit waited until one day when all the *Nish-na-bee* and *Mu-kaw-gee-yug* were out in the open fields. He commanded the four winds to come together more forcefully than they had ever blown before. The four winds swooped down and, taking turns, they picked up the *Nish-na-bee* and put them down gently here and there. And so began the separate tribes.

The same happened to the *Mu-kaw-gee-yug*, and that's why there are different breeds of dogs. Mother Nature always has the answers, if we trust and heed her wisdom.

Walk in Peace

PROGRESS

On a recent trip in northern Michigan I spent much time walking near the river and the edges of the swampland observing small frogs and water beetles. I noticed a school of bullheads with the protective parent nearby, staying close until they are large enough to go out by themselves.

The smell of the swampland, borne on the hot, humid air drifting through the tall pines, was overwhelming. Standing near the river, I envisioned my great-grandmother paddling her canoe through these waters. Now it is called the Inland Water Route and its banks are dotted with marinas, cottages, and houses. When it was cleared for use, the natural lay of the land and the wildlife was destroyed. The businessmen did not realize that along with their gain of water access came the destruction of the natural environment. As progress inched forward, it pushed the frontier of the animal people back. Their natural grounds and breeding places were replaced by houses, docks, and places of business.

Here, near the land of the Ottawa, Burt Lake Band, and *Shabo-e-guning* (Cheboygan) which means "going through," stood *Mu-kaw-gee* (Dog) and I, both of us absorbed in Mother Earth's wonders. As we sat *Au-dje-djawk* (Crane) flew by, its long legs trailing behind. I can still hear my Grandfather's words, "There goes

Johnny-up-the-creek" (so named because the bird was always heading upstream).

A noise interrupted my daydreaming. I looked up in time to see *Au-zhawshk* (Muskrat) cutting the water, heading for the opposite shore, probably to his home on the far bank. The harsh call of a gull screeched overhead, possibly heading out to Lake Huron for a feed.

Upstream lay docks with *Chi-mon-ug* (Boats) from 12 to 36 feet in length and motor-driven. This is a far cry from years past when these waters were only travelled by birchbark canoes that glided silently through pure waters.

Now the waters are polluted by man's refuse and garbage: tires, tin cans, and pieces of plastic. The bottom looks like a graveyard for man's discarded items. The water was no longer clear. I felt empty and sad. I wondered what *Maw-may* (Sturgeon), who has lived many snows, thought about the water. I can't help but feel that this polluted water must sting his eyes. I feel sorry for him. He has to endure but I'm sure he also has memories of these waters when they ran clean and clear.

Walk in peace

HOME LIFE

My wife, *Mony-qua* (Mary) and I were out doing our grocery shopping. On the way, we stopped in a little restaurant for a break and a cup of coffee. *Mony-qua* commented how quiet it was there and how good it was to be in such a peaceful atmosphere.

The conversation turned to the serenity of our home and how we could slow ourselves down by just looking out our dining room window at the fields. In our yard, there are several old apple trees, long past their productive years, but who stand out among the other trees as the Elders of their domain.

The soft, green grass is bisected by a path formed by *Waboose* (Rabbit) on his trip to our feeder. The path leads to enchanting fields. In the front of the house is a road, the main artery into town, on which cars whiz by at 45 or 50 mph. The speed limit is 35, but the drivers' minds are clouded and they do not see the signs; their goal is to get there in the least amount of time. Hurry and rush seems to be a chronic disease.

My Grandfather used to say, "Take your time, it'll keep." Somehow, as I have grown older, I know that the things he and *Seeson*, the medicine woman, said are true. Their philosophies were based on the old Indian way of living; be patient, accepting, and believing. It can be a simple way of life. What more can we ask for than Mother Earth's natural setting of beauty?

Traditionally, Indians start the day with thanks to the Great Spirit for another day. They accept the things that happen to them that day. Why not start the day off by looking to the East? Brother Sun will be coming out. Even if he is covered with clouds he is, in fact, there. Think positively and say, "It is a good day. I am alive and in good enough health to see Brother Sun come up."

My philosophy is based on what my Grandfather once told me. "Don't rush around, slow down. When you hurry to get something done or walk faster, you are hurrying yourself to your grave. Slow down and take your time." I believe this. These past years, I have practiced this philosophy. It is hard to do in a crowd, but you can set yourself apart from it.

Be good to yourself. It's easy when you enjoy the wonders of the Earth Mother.

Walk in Peace

James McCann 95
Ottawa

THE THREE LIVES

A long time ago, when Mother Earth was yet young, a little worm named *Mo-say* lived in the soft ground. Every once in awhile, he would poke his head out of the ground and look in amazement at the trees and shrubs, growing tall and short. *Mo-say* longed to stay up there but it was a strange world to him.

One day, he felt the ground shaking. When he poked his head above the ground he saw a strange shape. *Mo-say* wondered what it was. Suddenly the "thing" said, "Don't be afraid *Mo-say*. My name is *Nana-boo-shoo*. I am here to help you."

Mo-say was puzzled and asked, "Help me? Help me? Why?"

Nana-boo-shoo said, "Patience, little *Mo-say*. You'll see. In a few days, I want you to build yourself a warm nest and go to sleep, but make sure you have enough to eat."

So *Mo-say* ventured forth every day and fed on all the sweet roots he could find. One day while eating, he began to get sleepy. Remembering what *Nana-boo-shoo* had told him, he hurried to his nest and quickly pulled all the soft roots about him. Soon he was fast asleep.

As time passed, he grew within the nest. One day *Mo-say* woke up. He felt different. He stretched out, and noticed that now he had a covering on his skin. It was soft and fuzzy. He was black on each end, like the ground he crawled around in. The middle of him was a golden brown. He wanted to see what he looked like in the light above the ground, so he dug his way to the surface.

As *Mo-say* was looking at himself, *Nana-boo-shoo* came along, saw him and said, "What a beautiful coat you have, fuzzy black and brown like a Bear. Let's call you *Mo-seh* (Woolly Bear or Caterpillar)." So the first Caterpillar was created.

Mo-seh busied himself climbing all the trees and bushes that he had so admired. He munched many a day contentedly away on his favorite leaves. One day he saw some pretty red things on the branches of a bush and he went to explore. *Mo-seh* tried to climb up the slender stems, but they wouldn't support his weight. So down he went.

While *Mo-seh* was sitting there dejectedly, *Nana-boo-shoo* came along. He asked *Mo-seh*, "What's the matter?"

Mo-seh explained his longing to see the pretty red balls on the ends of the branches. *Nana-boo-shoo* told him, "Be patient, you'll get to see them. First though, you must do this. Again, you must eat plenty of food in order to get big and fat. Then from your mouth will come a fine, sticky string. Find a safe place and wind this around your body."

Mo-seh, remembering how nice his last change was, didn't hesitate and began to eat the tender leaves. Then he found a good spot way up in the tree and just like *Nana-boo-shoo* had commanded, he began to wrap the sticky string around himself. He then attached a string to a leaf and covered the rest of himself. Now there was only a sac hanging from the leaf.

Inside, *Mo-seh*, tired from spinning the sac, went to

sleep. Time passed and each day Brother Sun grew warmer. Still *Mo-seh* slept, but as he slept he was also growing. When *Mo-seh* woke up, he began to move around and because he now filled the sac entirely, it began to split. He wriggled and squirmed and crawled out of his sac home.

Brother Sun's warmth felt good. *Shaw-wah-nong* (South Wind) blew softly over him and said, "Welcome to Mother Earth. How beautiful you are."

Mo-seh didn't know what *Shaw-wah-nong* meant. He stretched again and then something wonderful happened. There were two strange things on his sides and they were slowly unfolding! *Mo-seh* saw that they were beautiful. They looked like the leaves he used to eat, thin and yet strong. Soon these pretty flaps were spread out.

Mo-seh wondered how he would crawl around with those two things stuck on him. As he sat wondering, *Shaw-wah-nong* (South Wind) blew hard and *Mo-seh* lost his hold and fell from the branch. As he fell, he spread out the leaf-like things and found himself gently gliding to Mother Earth. Safely on the ground, he began to move the 'leaves' gently, testing them. Soon they were moving together, and to his surprise he was again in the air! He realized that he could now go wherever he wanted.

Mo-seh spotted a pretty red flower and began to fly toward it. A sweet smell came from its center. He tried to get to the source of the sweet smell but the opening was too narrow. He stretched his head. Suddenly, his tongue unrolled. He tasted the sweet juice and found out he could drink it.

Then *Mo-seh* heard something. He looked up and saw *Nana-boo-shoo*. *Nana-boo-shoo* said, "What a beautiful thing you are. Let's call you . . . *May-may-gawn* (Butterfly)."

So from that day on, butterflies have passed through three stages to become adults. Their patience and obedience was rewarded by Mother Nature. Let us patiently heed Mother Nature; her order and system works so well. Haste has made our world a wasteland.

Walk in Peace

COMING OF AGE

Each culture has a "Coming of Age" ceremony to mark the transition into adulthood. Like the passing of so many Indian traditions, the rite of becoming a young man or a young woman has fallen by the wayside. Look at your own family and see how many traditions are carried on today. Think of the traditions your grandmothers and grandfathers used to perform on a daily or situational basis.

In my childhood, I had to go through the rituals of my people which were carried on from generation to generation. When I became thirteen years old, or as my Grandfather said, a "swamper," I realized why I had been taken on so many camping trips, taught how to identify fruits, berries, and leaves, how to build a fire, and where to place a camp.

What I had learned was now to be put to the test. I was to go into the woods for three days. My gear consisted of two blankets, a hatchet, a knife, a small kettle, flour, salt and a piece of bacon, and string and wire for snares and traps. These were my bare essentials. The rest was up to me. If I wanted to be accepted as a young man in the family and Indian community, I had to prove that the many trips had taught me something.

I was scared. What if I forgot some of the things that Grandfather had taught me? But Mother, with her knowledge of herbs, teas, and roots were a big comfort to me, and Dad, who had taught me where the natural resources were available and how to recognize signs of wildlife, made me feel secure. Now the payoff was near. Could I do it? There was no cutting corners or cheating. The Elders could recognize if you were lying about things of which they were so knowledgeable.

My test was to go ten miles into the woods the first day and prepare my lunch, which I had to catch or trap. Luckily I caught some brook trout. I wrapped them in burdock leaves, packed them in clay, and threw them into the fire to bake. Flour, water, and bacon fat mixed together, wrapped on a stick, and turned occasionally, furnished the bread. Wild strawberry leaves, steeped, made the tea. What a wonderful meal! I can still taste it. The aroma of the burning wood, the sweet smell of the earth, the chipmunks running around, and the chickadees hopping about, all lent tranquility to me.

After many hours of walking, I reached the place where I was told to go. I had to bring back the bark of a particular bush that only grew in that area as proof that I had been there. I set up camp. But I had no tent so I had to make a lean-to like I had made with Grandfather. I found a good spot, built the lean-to, then thought of supper. I took my slingshot and went stalking in the woods. Result: two robins, feathers for proof, and a meal. Baked robin, again packed in clay, berries and nuts, and bread on a stick was the wonderful reward.

The first day was coming to a close. I gathered enough firewood for the night and breakfast in the morning. I also remembered Grandfather talking of the bear and bobcat in this area. Later, I heard the bobcat crying and screaming and smelled the bear close by. The night noises were loud. What a way to become a man!

The second day consisted of a trip to a different part of the woods. There I was to find a hawk's nest and raid it, and bring back feathers and parts of the nest as proof. Then I needed to trap a rabbit and bring back the hide stretched on a frame. I had to use the wire to trap the rabbit because the hide could show no marks of a bullet or sharp object. It was tough to find a good runway and set the snare.

Breakfast consisted of baked bread on a stick, mashed berries for jam, nuts, and Sumac tea. Lunch was provided by *Waboose* (Rabbit). He gave his life for me to exist. I went through the ritual taught me by Grandfather, thanking the Great Spirit and Mother Earth for food. *Waboose* is my special friend; he is my clan sign. It is only fitting to use *Waboose*, my clan brother, to provide food and nourishment.

After carefully skinning the rabbit, I made a frame to stretch the hide. I had to provide my own frame. Remembering what my Grandfather had taught me, I gathered the supple red willow and quickly fashioned the frame. This was the proof needed by the Elders.

On my third day, there was another test to complete. I had to find some blue clay. But it was scarce in that part of the country. Then I remembered that Grandfather had showed me some blue clay while we were trapping mink. But how to get there from here was a problem. I found a tall pine tree, climbed it, took my bearings by the sun, and set out for the site of the blue clay. I crossed a river, went through a swamp, and found a creek. The underground stream gushed out of the side of the bank as if it was coming out of a six-inch pipe. There was lots of blue clay here. Grandfather could use this for the pottery in which he stored his different medicines.

The trip home was long. It seemed I would never get there. I was anxious to see my Mother, Dad, and Grandfather. Their approval was welcomed. I had fulfilled the test and I was now ready to enter manhood. My reward was an eagle feather from my Dad, tobacco from Grandfather, and a beaded band from Mother.

I have since lost the beaded band from my Mother; it was old and the thread was rotten with age. I tried to smoke the tobacco but it was too strong. I later found out it was meant for medicinal purposes and was not to be smoked.

I still practice some of those old traditions. I keep tobacco around and I still have the eagle feather that signifies I am a man. When I look at it, I remember my pleasant childhood.

When I talk to people of these things they listen to me, and deep inside I wonder how strange it must be not to grow up and enjoy Mother Earth and her natural resources.

Walk in Peace

POW-WOW

The Pow-Wow is one of the most misunderstood elements of modern Indian life. The non-Indian neither understands the importance of the Pow-Wow to the Indians nor why they cling to it and support it so deeply. To non-Indian people, the Pow-Wow is an opportunty for Indians to dance their native dances in leathers and buckskins. But to Indians the Pow-Wow is far more complex and ancient.

Generations ago, long before the Europeans came to the Americas, Indians lived happily and simply. There was purpose in their life. Indian men earned their status in the village either by competing in acts of bravery or hunting, or with their words of wisdom. The Indian women were known for their skill in preparing leather, making fur robes, cooking natural foods, and keeping the village in order. Their duties were delegated according to their skills. The women ruled the village with an iron hand; they were the backbone of the tribe. The Indian men depended on the women for their knowledge of village politics and they utilized that information in Council.

The Indians lived this way for centuries. But when the Europeans invaded, the Indians were overpowered and pushed back into smaller and smaller areas. The final result was total surrender. The conquerors dictated to the tribes that their old way of life could no longer be practiced or they would be charged with inciting war or plotting against the government.

The Indians, once a mighty race, retreated into their shell, beaten and conquered. Once proud warriors and braves, they were relegated to the life of a farmer and were told where to live. As the ways of the white man slowly took over, the Indian struggled to maintain his beliefs that he was part of nature, centered in Mother Earth. The old ways still smoldered in his very being. He was not giving up his birthright. Even though his clothes, housing, and life style were being changed, he clung to some basic customs.

Where once the Indian competed through his acts of bravery, prowess, and wisdom, now these were replaced with the Pow-Wow in which competition was expressed in the different dances, costumes, and the beat of the drum. This was the way he kept on being Indian. Attending a Pow-Wow became an act of cultural survival. Explaining this to a non-Indian is very hard because it is a concept that is older than the United States; part of the essence of the Indian's very existence. Now the Pow-Wow is a social, but serious, part of their lives.

The drum is the sacred center of Indian life. The drum head, once a living animal and a brother, furnishes the rhythm for the dance. The throbbing of the drum sends the spirit out into the bodies of the participants.

Hair, hawk, and eagle feathers flutter gracefully in the breeze. The hides of the animal brothers are adorned with beads, bones, and fringes.

The drum starts its rhythm. Quickly you step to its beat, trying to be better than your cousin. But you also watch the older men because they are better dancers, have better costumes, and their feathers and bead work is more beautiful. They are still proud warriors when they dance. They are carried back into time, back to when it was "INDIAN COUNTRY."

 Walk in peace

James McCammon 95
Ottawa

SWEET DISCOVERY

In the early spring, many people reminisce about making maple syrup. This always brings to mind the following story.

One day Chief *Muckwah-ne-bod* (Sleeping Bear) decided to go into the woods to hunt. He told his wife, *Wah-wah-tah-see* (Firefly), "I want a good supper of venison ready for me when I get back."

Wah-wah-tah-see watched her husband as he prepared for the hunt. She was proud of the eagle feathers he wore in his hair, the way he walked, and how he held himself so erect. She busied herself around the wigwam, doing the daily chores involved in housekeeping. When she finished her work, she decided to visit some of the other women in the village. They laughed and gossiped. *Wah-wah-tah-see* was enjoying herself so much she forgot that *Muckwah-na-bod* would be returning home from the hunt soon and would be hungry.

When *Wah-wah-tah-se* finally remembered she quickly ran home, built the fire, and put the venison in the pot. But when she reached for the water bag she found it empty! She didn't have time to go for water because the river was far from the wigwam.

What shall I do? How can I cook the venison with no water, she wondered. She was frightened of what *Muckwah-ne-bod* would do and say to her when he returned and found she did not have supper ready for him.

Then she thought of the Wise One. Perhaps he could help her. She hurried to the Wise One's wigwam and explained her carelessness. He shook his head and sadly said, "To be like the Cuckoo Bird does not become the wife of the Chief *Muckwah-ne-bod*. Return to your wigwam and cook your supper.

"But I have no water," cried *Wah-wah-tah-see*. The Wise One looked away and said, "The wife of *Muckwah-ne-bod* must find some water."

Realizing that the Wise One wouldn't help her, she ran into the woods. *Wah-wah-tah-see* tripped and fell to the ground and as she lay there she felt something like drops of rain of her head. She looked up and there, out of *Inina-atig* (Maple), was trickling a stream of water. She quickly fashioned a spout out of a piece of bark and put it in the tree with the water bag under the spout. She soon had enough water to cook the venison and she hurried home. The contents of the pot were soon boiling and a sweet odor filled the wigwam.

When it was time for *Muckwah-ne-bod* to return home *Wah-wah-tah-see* lifted the lid and looked in the kettle. Something was wrong! The 'water' had boiled away and the venison and kettle were both coated with small brown crystals. The strange sweet odor was one she had never smelled before. She suddenly became afraid that she had ruined the venison. Fearing what *Muckwah-ne-bod* would do to her, she ran into the woods to hide. Wandering about in the woods, she wept because of her carelessness. She told herself that she was not worthy to be the wife of a great chief.

Meanwhile, Chief *Muckwah-ne-bod* had returned home. Wondering where his wife had gone, he went to the pot where the venison was cooking. He sat down to enjoy supper.

Wah-wah-tah-see stayed in the woods until it was dark. Finally, she decided to go home and admit to her husband what she had done. She was sick with fear that he would be very angry. Instead, she found *Muckwah-ne-bod*, happily dipping his fingers in the kettle and licking the sticky liquid from them. He had eaten all the venison as well as the sugary crystals that clung to the sides of the kettle. *Muckwah-ne-bod* said, "Where did you get this?"

Wah-wah-tah-see dipped her own fingers into the kettle and put them in her mouth. Then she realized why her husband wasn't angry. The syrup on her fingers was delicious. Chief *Muckwah-ne-bod* was so pleased with the syrup that every spring he now ordered all the men and women of the village to catch the sap from *Inina-atig*.

Thus, through *Wah-wah-tah-see's* carelessness, she discovered syrup, sugar, and candy from the sap of the maple tree.

Walk in peace

THE BURNOUT

On March 28, 1836, a treaty was signed between the Ottawas and the government of the United States which ceded lands encompassing what is now the State of Michigan. Article 1 gave boundary lines for 16,000,000 acres of land. However, Article 2 is more interesting and is the subject of this essay.

The treaty clearly stated that tracts of land were to be held for the common use of Indians: one tract of 50,000 acres on Little Traverse Bay; one tract of 20,000 acres on the north shore of Grand Traverse Bay; one tract of 1,000 acres located by Chief *Chingassanee* (Big Sail) on the Cheboygan River; and one tract of 1,000 acres, located by *Mujeekewis* (West Wind) on Thunder Bay River. Stipulations, legal aspects, quit claim deeds, taxes, and other confusing issues became part of the day-to-day life of Indians. Legal terms were new to them and left them in a state of bewilderment. The Indians' interest lay in the earth and what she furnished for them to survive.

The Treaty of 1836 brought many Indians to the reservation lands that were set aside for them. The land of interest to this story lies in Cheboygan County, and encompasses some 411 acres which were settled in what is now Colonial Point (Indian Point) in Tuscorora Township on Maple Bay. Over 400 Indians lived in what was called the "Burt Lake Village."

Many people today have living relatives who can recall their mothers, fathers, aunts, and uncles talking of the burnout of Burt Lake Village in the fall of 1900. This incident has long been a thorn in the side of the Indians.

The potential of the land apparently influenced certain people to acquire it by any means possible. Non-Indians exploited the Indian's lack of knowledge about titles, taxes, and deeds. They managed to acquire the land in a technically legal, but unethical, way through tax sales and other legal loopholes. The Indians were instructed not to pay taxes because the land was being held in trust for them. But a local man acquired the land and started legal proceedings against the Indians. Now, where once the Indians had lived for nothing, they had to pay to live there.

On a cold October night in 1900, the Indians of Burt Lake Village were forcibly removed from their homes by the sheriff. They watched as their homes were set afire and all their possessions burned. They had nowhere to go. Some, including a 106-year-old woman, walked to Cross Village thirty-nine miles to the west. She died soon thereafter.

Children and relatives of that band can still recall the bitter memories and they are still saddened when they think of it. Most of all they resent the under-handed tactics which were used. It is said among the Indians that the sheriff, one of the people responsible for the burnout, went on to hold a high office in Lansing. It proves that men will go to great lengths to satisfy their greed for land and power, and that often good people found themselves on the wrong end of the deal.

It is a painful truth that in Michigan removal was in effect even after treaties were signed. The Burt Lake Village burnout influenced many Indian people to become more knowledgeable about the law. Now they use the laws made by white men to correct or get compensation for such incidents.

Today a rich resort has been built on the land where once Indians lived in their simple ways. Land where, on one bitter night in October, the air was filled with the acrid smoke of burning log houses and the possessions of the Indian people. Meanwhile the descendants of that village remember bitterly the events of that cold October night in 1900 on Indian Point on Burt Lake.

This incident brings back a memory from the my own past when I heard my Grandfather say, "When Indians won a battle it was a massacre, when the white man won a battle, it was a victory."

Walk in peace

INDIAN VETERANS OF THE CIVIL WAR

The movie *Roots* started a trend of people delving into their family history. Perhaps some weren't too pleased when they dug up family skeletons! Be that as it may, prior to *Roots* I had already done some research into my own family's history. From treaties, government Indian schools, politicians, and bureaus, I was able to learn a great deal about my family. Some of the information was given to me, little by little, by my Dad over his lifetime.

For those who are unfamiliar with Indian names and naming customs, an Indian was named early in his or her infancy. A proper name was bestowed with much pomp and dignity. It was a solemn occasion for the individual and to live up to the name could be difficult. The naming ritual was lost in the onslaught of European culture. It was a sad day for the Indian. Now he no longer has a name to live up to and his name is as common as the next man's.

My father told me that most name changes occurred during the Civil War when 64 Indians from Michigan served in the infantry and cavalry. The reason for the name change was due to the difficult pronunciation and complicated spelling of their names. To the best of my recollection, my grandfather's last name was *Kenui-ke-geshik* (Bird That Flies At Night). My Grandfather told my Dad that the names of the Indian soldiers were changed to names white men could pronounce and spell. Thus came about the last name of "Otto." People often comment that Otto is a German name. It is hard to explain to them that the history of my name is long and complicated.

Indian soldiers who served in the Civil War belonged to the Michigan Volunteers, Company F, 2nd Michigan Calvary and 2nd Michigan Infantry, 1st Sharpshooters Regiment. They were under the command of a half-breed, Lt. Graveret, who was said to be from the Leelanau Peninsula in the northwest part of lower Michigan in the land of the *Odawa* (Ottawa). Graveret died in 1864 from wounds received in action near Petersburg, Virginia.

My Grandfather fought in many campaigns during the Civil War, finally being wounded in the Battle of Mary's Heights where he lost an arm. He was mustered out and returned to his home on government trust land in Weidman, Michigan. He is buried there, somewhere in the northwest corner of the property, along with my Grandmother, his brother, and three of his children. I don't know, however, where my family's plot is located. The summer before he died, my father promised me he would show me where it was located, but he went on the "Long Walk" before he had time to keep his promise.

Strangely enough, when I went looking for information on the Sharpshooters Regiment in formal, written sources I found very little information. My Dad transmitted more information to me orally than did the "talking leaves" of the white men. But I had to be patient because if I prodded or asked too many questions of the Elders they would just stop talking and ignore me.

One of my Grandfather's greatest excuses was that he didn't want to disturb the sleep of his brothers as the wrath of *Nana-boo-shoo* would fall on us. His wise words carried a lot of weight because I was brought up to respect my elders.

Treaty rights are much discussed among Indian people. It seems strange to us that treaties were made and not kept especially when you consider that Indian men served, fought, and died for this country since its birth. Today there again rises the question of doing away with treaty rights.

I am a pacifist at heart, yet some of these things disturb me. There are too many greedy men, even today. I take no sides in the hassles concerning treaty rights. I sympathize with both sides because I've lived on both sides. Once I was an activist but now I am at peace with myself and all people.

Walk in Peace

James McCann 94
Ottawa

A CHANGE OF SEASON

Fall is the time of year when leaves turn beautiful shades of red, orange, yellow, and brown. What a gorgeous array of colors Mother Nature displays! They are all free for the viewing if one takes the time to stop and look. Combined with the light blue tinge of the sky and the dark blue-green of the lakes and rivers, a dazzling picture emerges, created by Mother Earth and assisted by the Great Spirit.

There are many scientific explanations of how and why the leaves turn colors in the fall. Some say the frost turns the leaves into different colors; others that the chlorophyll is leaving the leaves; and yet others that the natural food-juices from the trees have stopped, so it is natural for the leaves to die.

According to Indian legend the reason leaves change colors in the fall began a long time ago when *Nana-boo-shoo* made the trees and bushes. Although he had made flowers in all sizes, shapes, and fragrances, he realized something was wrong. He asked his faithful friend, *Mu-kaw-gee* (Dog), "What's wrong? They all look alike."

Mu-kaw-gee suggested they go to their favorite place on the hillside and think about it. So they went to the spot and were soaking in the warmth from Brother Sun when suddenly *Nana-boo-shoo* said, "I know! I'll make the flowers different colors. They shouldn't look like the trees and bushes."

So *Nana-boo-shoo* and *Mu-kaw-gee* began to think of the many possible colors they could make. They decided to use the bark and roots from the trees and shrubs to make the flowers different colors. While they were thinking about it, they became sleepy and were soon fast asleep.

Upon waking, *Nana-boo-shoo* noticed that daylight was fading fast and wanting to finish before dark, he quickly mixed the colors in pots. He strapped the pots on *Mu-kaw-gee* and he started to paint the flowers. He hurried from one flower to another, splashing the colors carelessly on the leaves of the trees and shrubs in the fields and woods around him in the process. When they finished, *Nana-boo-shoo* and *Mu-kaw-gee* turned around and were surprised to see that both the flowers and the trees were painted in different hues.

Nana-boo-shoo said to *Mu-kaw-gee*, "It is good. From now on when *Pee-boon* (Winter) is getting ready to arrive, the trees and bushes will change color. This will alert the birds and animal brothers of what is to come."

So from that day forth, the leaves and trees change colors in *Tay-gwan-gee* (Fall). When you notice the first leaf has turned, remember that *Nana-boo-shoo* and *Mu-kaw-gee* have begun their painting spree.

Walk in peace

HAPPENINGS OF MOTHER EARTH

According to the traditions and customs of the Indian world the beginning of a new year is based on the seasons of Mother Earth and the cycles of Grandmother Moon. According to the Gregorian calendar, by March one-fourth of the year is already past. But in the world of the Indian, the new year begins when the snows of winter leave and new life springs from Mother Earth. Then all plant and animal life on Mother Earth begins to awake in a surge of new life and energy under the warm breezes from the south (*Shaw-wah-nong*), and the rains from the west (*A-pung-ish-a-moog*). Brother Sun provides the sunlight for the new growth of trees and plants.

This rebirth is the gift of the Great Spirit. The mild south winds instill new life in the birds who return by instinct from their wintering grounds. The sap from the maple trees is straining to escape. Restless fish stir and begin to return to the rivers and lake beds where they started life to create new life.

The Great Spirit commands fresh hope and as each new bud on the branches swells, one can almost feel, day-by-day, the urgency of the rebirth. Today, a friend visited and left some pussywillows for my family. What a good feeling to see these fresh wisps, part of Mother Earth's courage. What perfection in the catkins! Even the uneven branches are artistically perfect.

But after *Ne-bin* (Summer) comes the first hint of *Tau-gwan-gee* when *Nana-boo-shoo* will paint the ground white with frost and the trees with red and gold. Soon the *Ke-way-di-noong* (Cold North Winds) will bring a mantle of white to usher in the long sleep for the plants and some animals of the forests.

One year (or one snow) is measured by 13 full moons from which came the expression "many moons." Brother Sun was also a measure of time, marking the beginning of each new day; which journey in turn shows the time of the day itself.

The Indian of old had much reverence for Mother Earth. His existence depended on the weather. If the weather wasn't cooperative then rituals and offerings were made to the Great Spirit. However, the life of the Indian today is about the same as anyone else's save that the most of them are still Indian at heart. May their moccasins always walk light and walk on the smooth, cool earth of the pine forests.

Mother Earth is our calendar, our watch, our provider, our shelter. It is my hope you will enjoy with me, her wonders.

Walk in peace

NAMES OF MONTHS

The Indian's year is different from his white brother's year. The Indian is attuned to Mother Earth and his year follows the seasons. Indian cultural and religious beliefs were centered around the moon, sun, and the elements. The months of the Indians were based on Grandmother Moon because she appeared every 28 days without fail. The Indians also noted the behavior of animals and the growing season. Some months are named for ripening berries, some for other happenings in the lives of animals.

This particular version of the how the months acquired Indian names comes from the maternal side of my family tree from a distant cousin of *Odawa* (Ottawa) descent, and a member of the Grand River Band of Ottawas.

Here is a list of months according to Indian tradition:

December
Muh-koo-gee-sis (Ottawa)
Bear Moon
Man-i-doos-gee-sis (Chippewa)
Little Spirit Moon

January
Man-i-do-gee-sis (Ottawa)
Spirit Moon

February
Nuh-mah-be-ne-gee-sis (Ottawa)
Sucker Moon

March
Zis-bok-wa-to-ke-win (Ottawa)
Sugar-Making Moon

April
Ba-boo-quad-ah-gimping (Ottawa)
Snowshoe Breaking
Ne-ke (Chippewa)
A wild goose
Sagi-ba-ga (Chippewa, Northern Minnesota)
Leaves come forth

May
Wah-be-goo-neh (Ottawa)
Flowers
Sagi-ba-ga (Chippewa, Northern Minnesota)
Leaves come forth

June
O-dae-mi-ne (Ottawa)
Strawberry Moon

July
Mis-qua-mi-ne (Ottawa)
Raspberry
Mee-nun (Ottawa, Lower Michigan)
Blueberry
Pa-pashk-is-ige (Chippewa)
Shooting Moon (Fourth of July)

August

Mee-nun (Ottawa, Upper Michigan)
Blueberry
Muh-no-min-keh (Ottawa, Upper Michigan)
Blueberry
Muh-no-min-keh (Chippewa, Wisconsin & Minnesota)
Rice Gathering
Wa-teh-ba-ga (Chippewa)
Leaves Changing Color

October

Pen-ah-que (Ottawa)
Falling Leaves
Pe-nah-kwaw-we (Chippewa)
Freezing
Meek-wahm-ke (Chippewa)
Ice-Making Moon

There has never been an agreement on the spelling of the months. Some months have the same name as the last month because at times there is a longer season than in some of the other months.

The year begins for the Indian when the snows leave and life springs anew from Mother Earth to begin a whole new cycle of life and growth. Despite of the predictions of weathermen, we are still at the mercy of the Mother Earth. I accept this. Even when I weary of the elements, I know that one day Brother Sun will again shine down with his life-giving warmth, and all this will be only a memory.

Walk in Peace

James McCann 94
Ottawa

TALE OF THE TAMARACK

The Tamarack (*Au-ke-kaw-daw*) is a species of larch tree. Its wood is rarely used as lumber because of its hardness and wild grain, but it did serve as beams for barns and logs for houses. The Indians hardly used this tree at all, because they believed this legend connected with *Au-ke-kaw-daw*.

A long time ago the Great Spirit created Mother Earth. All the trees, bushes, and plant life had been put in their own places, and the Great Spirit was satisified with each one.

After creating plant life the Great Spirit was tired and decided to rest. He picked a spot on the side of a hill and was looking over the many different trees and shrubs he had created when he heard someone talking. He followed the sounds of speech and found *Au-ke-kaw-daw*. *Au-ke-kaw-daw* was talking to *Inina-atig* (Maple). *Au-ke-kaw-daw* was envious of *Inina-atig's* large, flat leaves and said, "How come the Great Spirit gave you large leaves and gave me none?"

Inina-atig did not know what to say. He answered cautiously, "We should not question the Great Spirit's actions and decisions."

Au-ke-kaw-daw, still disgruntled, looked around and saw *Wig-wasi* (White Birch). He asked *Wig-wasi*, "How come the Great Spirit gave you white bark? Why didn't he give it to me?"

The stately *Wig-wasi*, satisfied and proud said, "We should all be happy we are here."

The Great Spirit, hearing *Au-ke-kaw-daw's* complaints, said to *Au-ke-kaw-daw*, "Why are you dissatisfied?"

Au-ke-kaw-daw complained to the Great Spirit, "*Inina-atig* has bigger leaves than I have and *Wig-wasi's* skin is white and smooth. Why can't I have those things?"

The Great Spirit was perturbed with *Au-ke-kaw-daw* and said, "They have to have something special of their own. I don't hear them complaining. You have a nice straight body, your wood is hard and can be used for many things, and your needles are green and lacy. What more do you want?"

Au-ke-kaw-daw thought about what the Great Spirit said. He thought, *I guess I am different from the other trees at that.*

But as time went by, *Au-ke-kaw-daw* again found himself looking enviously at the other trees. He looked at the mighty *Shin-gwawk* (Pine) and said, "How come you're tall enough to reach the sky and you have long, green needles?"

Shin-gwawk said, "Perhaps I am sitting in a place where I can grow fast and the food and nourishment are just right. Stretch out your branches, maybe you can grow tall with long, green needles, too."

Au-ke-kaw-daw tried in vain to stretch out his branches. While he was doing so, he noticed a large Beech tree (*Aw-shaw-way-nish*). Animals were gathering nuts from the Beech.

Au-ke-kaw-daw asked *Aw-shaw-way-nish*, "The Great Spirit gave you nuts with which to feed the animals. Why didn't he give them to me?"

The Great Spirit was tired of *Au-ke-kaw-daw's* complaints. He said angrily, "From this day on you will be like *Shin-gwawk* and *Inina-atig* in some respects. Your wood will only be good for beams, you shall have needles, but you shall lose them when *Ke-way-di-noong* (Cold North Wind) comes. When the wind blows through your barren branches you shall cry."

Thus, *Au-ke-kaw-daw*, because of his jealousy and complaining, lost out in the end; he is condemned to stand a lonely vigil in the swampland.

Walk in Peace

MOTHER EARTH'S MESSENGERS

"*Mino gijigad.*" "It is a fine day." Our brothers, the animals, tell us long before the weather forecasters that the weather will warm up. Last week I observed *Essikon* (Brother Raccoon), *Kagons* (Brother Porcupine), and *Au-pe-tchi* (Brother Robin) who were foraging for food and choosing mates for the year to come. The urge of the mating season is as old as the world itself; a purpose set down by the Great Spirit.

The fowl of the wilds have shown up too. It is a sad day for *Pe-nay* (Brother Partridge). He was hit by *Da-bon* (Car). *Pe-nay* is not used to flying near the road. Although he flies among the trees and can fly around them he doesn't know that the car moves. Thus, many birds are killed by the machines that move; it is not part of their life. They are confused when they enter the realm of the human; it is all scary and new to them. Some do not make it back to warn their brothers of the dangers of man.

We'we (Brother Goose) is on his long journey to the land of *Giwedin* (the North) where he will pick a mate and vie for the role of leader of the flock. As their leader he will take them back south. He too has a job to do.

If it is truly warm *Ginebig* (Brother Snake) will come out. He's always cold and his skin is wet to the touch, so Brother Sun is a special friend to him.

Omakoki (Brother Frog) is also out at night, singing and looking for a mate. He has spent the winter burrowed deep in the mud of the lake and streams. The Great Spirit gave him special equipment to live on land and also breathe in the water. Lucky *Omakoki*!

Ke-gon-ug (Fish) are heavy with eggs and their spawning run is starting. One of the first is *Maw-maw-bin* (Sucker). He is easy to catch; he eats anything. Bony he is, but also tasty.

All these awakenings are a part of the cycle of life here on Mother Earth. Each season brings a new aspect whether it be spring, summer, fall or winter. Each season was made for a purpose and a different phase of our brothers the animals.

Sometimes I hear someone say "poor animals." They are not poor; they accept what is there. They suffer little pain and they are equipped with their own pain killers. We are not so fortunate; we have to work and forage more than they do. We are spoiled by mechanization and substitute food laced with man-made chemicals. It is mankind who should be pitied, not the animals.

Walk in peace

BIRTH OF FOG

Weather forecasters predicted heavy snow this winter, but Mother Nature didn't cooperate. I trust the built-in weather forecasting abilities of my *Mu-kaw-gee-yuks* (Dogs). The system that the Great Spirit gave these 'weather dogs' is pretty accurate. Now I see why *Nana-boo-shoo* chose as his favorite companion, *Mu-kaw-gee*, who is not only a true and faithful friend, but also a weather barometer and long-range weather oracle.

Most Indians accept all kinds of weather because they know there is not much they can do about the whims of the Great Spirit. So why even question it? For instance, many mornings of late there have been heavy fogs that have caused concern to drivers who must travel through almost zero visibility. Indians accept fog as a gift from the Great Spirit and tell a story about its birth.

One day *Kee-wa-zee* (Old Man) and *Du-moo-ya-quay* (Old Woman) were debating what to have for their supper. After much talking and bickering, they decided to have *Kee-go* (Fish) because they knew that at this time of the year the flesh of *Maw-maw-bin* (Sucker) would firm and tasty. *Maw-maw-bin* would also be plentiful in the streams because they were on their way to spawn. This journey was their role on the Earth Mother.

Kee-wa-zee and *Du-moo-ya-quay* decided to move their camp to the creek where they could harvest *Maw-maw-bin* easily. There they would roast, dry, and smoke the flesh of *Maw-maw-bin* and trade it with the young braves in the village. The young braves were skilled in hunting and had plenty to barter with *Kee-wa-zee* and *Du-moo-ya-quay*.

Kee-wa-zee and *Du-moo-ya-quay* made camp near the cedars where the creek seemed to be the best for harvesting the fish. In the morning they cleaned *Maw-maw-bin*, and gathered firewood for smoking the flesh. They gathered the boughs of the cedars and placed them on the flames–not enough to put it out, but enough to cause it to smoke. As they caught and cleaned the fish they smoked the flesh over the smoldering fire. This they did for several days, as they wanted a good supply for trading.

Finally, when they had enough smoked *Maw-maw-bin* they broke camp, smothered the fire, and left for the village. As they reached high ground, they turned around and saw the smoke from their camp fire hanging over the swampland. Thus, the first fog was seen by *Kee-wa-zee* and *Du-moo-ya-quay*.

Walk in Peace

INDIAN SPIRITUAL WORLD

Today, among the three major tribes of Michigan exist different religions. The Jesuit missionaries, traveling with the fur traders, introduced European culture and religion. The settlers also brought their ministers to administer the Word. So it was that many forms of religion were introduced to the Indian world in an effort to convert the "savages."

The Indian had his own religion in which he reverenced the land, trees, and animal life. The whole of Mother Earth was his church. The Indian only had to look around him to know that the Great Spirit was there in some form or that it was created by him. He did not have to travel far to worship, it was there at every turn in the trail, in every animal. He knew from these things there was a beginning, a supreme being, or Great Spirit. He knew that there was a purpose in his life and that everything was put here for a reason. It was up to him to use them properly.

The medicine man was the spiritual head of a tribe or band. The medicine man began at an early age to learn his craft. He was knowledgeable in the arts of healing and used incantations (prayers) to ask the Great

Spirit to the heal the sick and those believed to be possessed by evil spirits. It is said that he could contact the spirit world and seek aid from a spirit. He could ensure good crops, a good hunt, or success in wars. He had to be soothsayer, magician and, oftentimes, a hypnotist. He performed the rituals and asked for guidance from the Great Spirit. In Council his advice was sought out and highly respected.

Today, in and around Michigan, there are only a few medicine men left. Their role has been taken over by other forms of religion. The Indians have accepted the ways of the dominant society, but yet they still believe in some of the old ways. These beliefs are more prevalent in the Elders of the tribes because they can remember the times of old, the use of many remedies, and the old beliefs. Most are caught between modern day beliefs and religion, yet still retain remnants of the ancient beliefs.

In many places of business, one can find the Indian Prayer,

Grant that I may not criticize my neighbor,
until I have walked a mile in his moccasins.

There is another prayer in which I have found much comfort. It has no name or author and it goes something like this:

O Great Spirit,
whose voice I hear in the winds,
and whose breath gives life to all the world.
Hear me! I am small and weak, I need your
strength and wisdom.

Let me walk in beauty, and make my eyes
ever behold the red and purple sunset.
Make my hands respect the things you have made and my
eyes and ears sharp to hear your voice.

Make me wise so that I may understand
the things you have taught my people.
Let me learn the lessons you have hidden
in every leaf and rock.

I seek not strength, not greater than my brother,
but to fight my greatest enemy—myself.
Make me always ready to come to you with
clean hands and straight eyes.
So when life fades, as the fading sunset, my spirit may
come to you without shame.

My respect and thanks to the one who composed such meaningful thoughts about the world as seen through the eyes of the Indian.

Walk in Peace

James McCann 94
Ottawa

THE FIRST BEAVER

There once was a boy called *Chi-wa-bik* (Big Tooth) who near a beautiful lake whose waters were pure and clean. He spent many hours playing near the lake. One day his curiosity got the better of him and he asked his grandfather from whence came the waters of the lake. His grandfather replied that it came from underground rivers and feeder streams that emptied into the lake.

Now *Chi-wa-bik* wasn't satisfied with this answer so he sought out information from other Elders of his village. Soon he became a nuisance and a pest because of his questions. Seeking out many sources was not the way of the Indian and many adults and Elders talked of the boy who asked too many questions.

One day the medicine man stopped *Chi-wa-bik* and told him that to go against the ways of old was bad, and strange things would happen to him if he continued. But, despite the warning from the medicine man, *Chi-wa-bik* still asked questions.

Chi-wa-bik was so enchanted by the beautiful lake that he selfishly wanted it all for himself. But the law of the village was to share and *Chi-wa-bik,* seeing all the people on the edges of the lake, knew that he had to go elsewhere. One day *Chi-wa-bik* decided to seek out the source of the lake waters. He packed a supply of food in his canoe and paddled out into the lake. He chose one of the larger streams and followed it to its source.

When he arrived at the source of the waters of the lake he saw that the area was as beautiful as the lake itself. He thought, *I'll stop the water and make my own lake, all for myself.*

He looked for the best spot to stop the water and he put small sticks across the stream and packed them in with clay. Then he walked over the clay to form a packed base. He became so entranced with building his own lake that he worked from sunup to sundown.

The lake behind the dam was getting larger and larger and it required bigger sticks and more clay to keep it at bay. He began to work twice as hard. The larger the lake became, the more trees he had to haul. The more trees that were needed the farther he had to go to cut them down, the harder he had to swim to float them in place, and the more clay he needed to pack them in.

One day while gloating over his new lake a strange feeling came over him. He looked down at himself and realized that he had turned into *Au-mick*, the beaver! So the warning of the old medicine man had come true! Now he had his own lake, teeth with which to cut down trees, webbed feet for swimming, and a flat tail with which to pack the mud and clay. Now he had to be content with making the lakes and rivers his home for the rest of time.

The Great Spirit creates life and each animal for a reason. Selfishness made *Chi-wa-bik* into *Au-mick* the beaver.

Walk in peace

A VISIT WITH THE ANIMAL BROTHERS

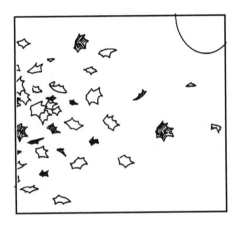

Hints of *Tau-gwan-gee* (Fall) are in the air. The cool nights, the shorter days, Brother Sun coming up later and going down earlier are all indications of *Tau-gwan-gee*. *Ne-bin* (Summer) is getting old and the *No-won-yaw* (Air) is cooling off.

The brothers of the woods and air also know because the Great Spirit gave them each a particular sense of being able to foretell the change of the seasons. Come take a walk with me among the wonders of Mother Earth and her children.

As we pass the river, *She-sheb* (Duck) is now a mother of five. Just a short while ago she was sitting on her nest and now her young are ready to fly. They will need strong wings to make the long trip to the South. *She-sheb* flies a little and her ducklings try to follow her. Again she flies a little and stops. The ducklings try again, half running, half flying over the water. Soon, they will be flying with their mother. In *Me-nou-kaw-me* (Spring) they will return to begin another cycle of life.

In a nearby tree the light tapping of Nuthatch can be heard. He is after the *Maw-ne-ton-ug* (Insects) that live just under the bark. The Nuthatch is the acrobat of the bird world because he can walk down a tree head first. He also seems to use his tail for a chair while picking out bugs.

Tchin-dee (Bluejay) is visiting again. His incessant hollering is sweetened by the sight of his beautiful blue, gray, and black feathers. *Tchin-dee* and *Awn-daya* (Crow) are the sentinels of the woods. Many times I've mumbled a few choice words for both of them, not realizing they were looking out for the other brothers of the woods.

A big black walnut (*Paw-gaw-naw-ko-paw-gon*) grows across the road. *Au-saw-naw-go* (Squirrel) lives there. He has been busy storing his food supply and breaking open the cones of *Ga-wan-dag* (Spruce) in the yard for the seeds. He sits in the Cedar (*Kezhek*) and chews off the tender seed pods. Down the street is a *Au-zhaw-way-mish* (Beech tree). Soon *Au-saw-naw-go* will be busy collecting the delicious beech nuts.

The berry season is drawing to a close but the last blackberries are still hanging on. The gooseberries, sugar plums, and raspberries are all gone. *Maw-kwa* (Bear) has been getting his share of them: he too knows that *Pee-boon* (Winter) is coming.

Along the edges of the lakes are remnants of wild cranberries. Pleasant memories come back of when I went picking cranberries with Mother and Dad long ago. *Chi-mon* (Boat) goes by. The fisherman have been seeking *Kee-go* (Brother Fish). *Kee-go* is smart: he is staying in the deep water until it cools off.

Somewhere in the distance a locust is singing in the trees. This is a sure sign of approaching *Tau-gwan-gee*. The Martins and Swallows have all gone. It seems like yesterday I watched them build their nests. *Ozaw-waw bine-shan* (Brother Canary), a seed eater, is here again. There is lots of food for him.

High above the tranquility is broken. A jet flies by leaving a trail of vapor where once *Wing-ge-zee* (Mighty Eagle) flew.

Walk in Peace

James McCann 95

BROTHER SKUNK'S PUNISHMENT

A long time ago when Mother Earth was young, man and the animals could talk with each other. They greeted each other with good will; neither had to defend himself from each another because all creatures and things were compatible on Mother Earth.

It wasn't until much later, when man had not followed the suggestions of the Great Spirit, that man and his animal brothers were punished by losing their gift of mutual respect. Now man had to fear his animal brothers and in return the animal brothers would have to defend themselves. So they began to keep their distance from each other; they were not friends anymore but rather friendly enemies. Now, because man used animals as food and their skins to make rawhide and leather for clothing, the animals developed an extra awareness; they were always alert to man's presence.

Chee-ma-gute (Brother Skunk) had no defense from man because there had been no need. But now the ties had been broken. Suddenly, man had become his adversary. What could he do to defend himself?

Chee-ma-gute went to the Great Spirit and asked for some form of defense from man. Anything would be better than this awful helplessness. So the Great Spirit gave *Chee-ma-gute* sharp claws. *Chee-ma-gute* looked at the long, sharp claws and tried to walk with them.

"They make me look awkward and the other animals will laugh at me," he complained to the Great Spirit.

So the Great Spirit took the claws away and gave *Chee-ma-gute* long teeth. Again, *Chee-ma-gute* complained that the long teeth made him look funny. Now the Great Spirit was getting perturbed with *Chee-ma-gute* because he was nit-picking about what the Great Spirit gave him.

"I shall give you one more chance," said the Great Spirit. "You are harder to please than your other animal brothers."

He gave *Chee-ma-gute* the ability to run so fast he could outrun most any animal around. Again, *Chee-ma-gute* complained, "If I am able to run that fast, nobody will be able to see my beautiful black-and-white coat."

The Great Spirit was disgusted with Skunk. He had tried to help him three times and each time Skunk wasn't satisfied. He told him, "Since you wanted everything your own way and didn't like the things I gave you to defend yourself with, I'll give you something that you and all your brothers shall remember you by."

Chee-ma-gute, happy now because he thought he was going to have a defense that was truly his own, was overjoyed. The Great Spirit said, "Here, take this bag and when somebody comes near you that you don't like, squeeze it and they'll leave." So *Chee-ma-gute*, happy with the new form of defense, left.

As he was going home he met *Mu-kaw-gee* (Dog). Now *Mu-kaw-gee* never even thought to bother *Chee-ma-gute*. However, as they walked by each other, *Chee-ma-gute*, curious, squeezed the bag. Phew!! What an odor!! Even *Chee-ma-gute* didn't like it.

Mu-kaw-gee ran away and rolled in the sand and on the ground to get rid of the smell. *Mu-kaw-gee* quickly told the other animals. From that day on because *Chee-ma-gute* didn't like the defenses the Great Spirit first gave him, he had no friends because of his terrible smell.

Now *Chee-ma-gute* only travels at night because he's ashamed of himself for refusing the protection first offered him by the Great Spirit. So when you see this little black-and-white animal of the night, remember he wanted his own way, and ended up alone among his wiser animal brothers.

Walk in Peace

THE OLD VILLAGE

When my great-grandmother was a very young girl she visited, with her mother and father, many villages on the shores of Lake Michigan. This is a story of one village and how my Dad, and later myself, began the search for it and of its meaning to us.

Before World War II, my Dad would pack some food and a bedroll and leave late on a Saturday night. I was very small at the time but I can remember the preparation for his excursions. I would watch as he packed a shovel, small pick axe, and an axe and I would often wonder what and where these trips led him. My Dad assured me that some day I could go with him. My Mother often accompanied him and they would bring back artifacts that apparently led them to believe they were nearing their quest.

Once my brother and I were taken on one of these trips. On the long walk through woods and over trails my Mother and Dad stopped often to show us plants and explain how they were used. My Mother would cook over the fire and often under the ashes as well, using the ground as a natural oven.

The fresh air off the lake, the sweet smell of the woods, and the many sightings of animal life were all part of these explorations. For my brother and I it was a chance to get out, for we were natural explorers at heart. We watched the raccoons in the creeks searching for food. Once in a while we would see an eagle in its mighty flight, and one time we were rewarded by the aerial acrobatics of these mighty birds. The eagles would fly way up into the sky until they were the size of dots. Then they would begin their play, diving at one another and becoming one, tumbling over and over toward the ground, until at the last moment they would part and pull out of their dive, climbing again high into the sky. My Dad said, "They are not playing but fighting to establish territorial rights."

My Dad continued his search over many years. One day on his return he produced a skull he had dug up. He told my Mother that he was sure he had found the site of the village. He announced that the following week we would all go in search of the village. The skull was sent to the archaeological department of a university where it was subjected to Carbon 14 tests to determine its age. Meanwhile, the search for the village went on.

One day while on a dig, we were in the area where Dad had found the skull. We discovered a cemetery or graveyard, but there was no way to tell how many graves were on the site. Realizing we were on sacred ground, and out of respect for our ancestors, we moved further to the west where there was a small creek teeming with trout.

There Dad walked around looking for telltale signs of the vanished village. He came to a halt and showed us a depression in the earth and told us to stand there. He started to follow the deep depression. Periodically he hollered and, following his instructions, we answered him. He made a complete circle about 100 feet in width. He came back and said, "We've found the village."

The depression was about 3 feet across and about 12 inches deep. It was a dance circle used by the Indians for their many dances, religious rituals, and ceremonies. We stood in the middle of the village, now grown over with pine trees, poplar, tag alders, and underbrush. We dug down about 2 feet and found remnants of pottery, stone tools, arrowheads, campfire ashes, and chips of flint. At long last the village was discovered!

My dad dug in the village for a couple more years. It became a form of relaxation for him; he lived for each weekend and the dig at the village. Then a disaster happened. Workmen with the saws, axes, and bulldozers put a rough road right through the middle of the cemetery and village. When World War II broke out all construction stopped, but not before the ground was torn up and all signs of the village were destroyed. All the years of searching and digging were gone in a few short weeks.

Meanwhile, the results of the carbon 14 tests on the skull came back. The skull had belonged to a female child about eight years old, who had apparently died from a blow to the back of the head which was indicated by a small hole in the back of the skull. The skull was about 400 years old, placing the existence of the village at around 1540 AD.

Today when I drive through that particluar area, I think of my early childhood. Now there is a nuclear plant, small factories, and plush houses where once there was peaceful tranquility. But many memories of happenings and stories rush back to me.

Today the lake looks the same as it did then and the same creek still flows but now with only an occasional trout. Civilization now stands where once there flourished part of the Indian nation.

Walk in Peace

REBIRTH

It was about the time when the Great Spirit was creating the animals and fishes, and putting them in places in and around the lakes, forests, and countryside that this particular story came to be.

Jo-bee (Muskrat) lived alone in a big lake, far away from the other muskrats. He was always grumpy and mean. He had no friends because of his disposition, nor did he particularly care for any.

He built his house of twigs, grass, and branches near the place where a small creek flowed out of the lake. *Jo-Bee* wanted to block up the creek so the water wouldn't escape but each time he put small twigs there the pressure from the water would wash them away. *Jo-Bee* thought, *If only there was some way I could get bigger branches and small trees to block the creek, then it would slow the waters down.*

One day as *Jo-Bee* sat pondering on how to fell a tree an idea came to him. He picked a small tree and started to gnaw at it with his back teeth. He kept it up, changing from one side of his mouth to the other. Eventually he grew tired of chewing so he rested a minute. When he started again he used his front teeth so he could give the sides of his mouth a rest. He began he notice that he was chewing into the tree faster than he had before, and the chips were bigger. He went to the lake and looked at himself in the water's reflection. He saw that his teeth had become long and sharp!

Jo-Bee was so busy looking at his new teeth in the water he didn't notice that a strong wind had come up. The wind blew so hard that the tree he had been gnawing on crashed to the ground, falling across his tail, which was long and round. Now the falling tree had flattened his out his tail! *Jo-Bee* quickly put his new, flat tail into the cool mud to soothe the pain.

He kept putting his flattened tail into the mud each day until it was no longer sore. He gave the mud a few pats with his tail to thank it for its healing and soothing powers. In doing so he noticed that with each pat the mud was being packed down.

Jo-Bee had an idea. With his long, sharp teeth he would cut the trees, and with his tail he would pack mud in between the trees, branches and twigs. In this way he could create a dam to hold the water in his lake. So having turned misfortune into a good fortune, the grumpy *Jo-Bee* turned into the *Chi-wa-bik* (Beaver).

Walk in peace

THE RAID

Among natural food buffs and nature lovers it is said that honey is one of Mother Nature's most perfect foods. Honey is a natural sweetener produced by the honey bees. Scientists remain baffled as to how the bees produce honey. It is yet another wonder of Mother Earth that we accept without giving it a second thought.

The Indians had natural sweeteners like maple sugar and honey. When liquid maple sugar is poured into molds and cooled it becomes maple sugar candy. When I was growing up, there were door-to-door peddlers who sold fruit, eggs, milk, meat, and sometimes, honey. Mother used to buy honey in the comb and we would spread it on fresh baked bread. That serves to bring to mind the following adventure.

Once, while out running the trap line with my Grandfather, I noticed a ball of wild honey bees on a tree limb. I brought it to the attention of my grandfather. He promptly sat down, took out his pipe, loaded it and commenced to smoke silently.

Grandfather was a man of few words, but when he spoke he said a lot. I asked him, "What are the bees doing?" He said, "They're moving to a new home, we'll watch them."

After an hour the bees moved and we followed them to a hollow poplar tree which was to be their new home. It was early May and Grandfather told me that in *Tau-gwan-gee* (Fall) we would come back and harvest the honey. In November, Grandfather and I visited the honey tree. We arose early one Saturday morning while it was still dark, loaded our gear, and headed for the woods. The air was nippy and there was frost on the ground. Grandfather said, "Just right for us."

We arrived at the tree near daylight. Grandfather began to saw on the tree. All I could think of was being stung by the bees. Grandfather wasn't concerned though. All he said was, "We won't get stung!"

Indeed, the bees came out but they just fell to the ground. I asked Grandfather, "What's the matter with the bees?" Grandfather explained that animals and bees go into a state of hibernation and are not active during the cold months of winter.

Soon the tree lay on the ground and the bees were trying to crawl out. Grandfather started to saw again just above where the bees were emerging. Mother Nature continued to work against the bees as the cold frosty air left them immobile. What a relief! We wouldn't get stung.

Soon the hollow log was cut through and the bees tumbled out onto the ground. Grandfather took a stick and brushed out the remaining bees to expose the combs of honey. He scooped it up with a small paddle and filled a pail half full. He commented, "Lots of honey, long winter."

Grandfather propped the tree up and tenderly gathered the bees and put them back in the nest. He plugged the cut end with birch bark and sealed it with pitch from a tree. He said, "Good as new, they'll be all right."

On a warm day in late March I visited the tree. The bees were stirring, ready to start another colony. I was happy because I thought we had destroyed their home. Later, in May, I noticed that the tree had been abandoned. The bees had moved to another location. I later found the new honey tree but I kept the information to myself because I knew how hard and time-consuming it was for the bees to relocate, rebuild, and pick a leader.

If one really looks at nature, you can seen that each and every things had a unique quality of its own; this in itself is a miracle of the Great Spirit.

Walk in peace

THE COMING OF WINTER

The leaves of the trees have fallen, covering Mother Earth, and the animals of the forests have sought out their places to sleep. The naked trees look like sentinels. Winter is one of the happenings of Mother Earth and is part of the Great Spirit's plan. Everything must rest and so it is with Mother Earth in the Winter. The trees, grass, flowers, bushes, and plants all take a well-earned sleep.

And so it was that there once lived a very old, very grouchy man in the north country who we shall call *Pee-boon* (Winter). He had no friends because the air around him was always cold, the water and ground became hard, and when he breathed white fluffy stuff came from his breath. *Pee-boon* also made it a habit to stay for a long time.

Muk-kwa (Brother Bear) knew when *Pee-boon* would be coming because his appetite would grow. Because *Muk-kwa* didn't want to be around when *Pee-boon* came, he would look for a place to hide and go to sleep. The animals that didn't go to sleep didn't like *Pee-boon* because food was scarce and his cold breath killed all the berries and leaves forcing them to dig in the deep snow for food.

Kee-go (Brother Fish) didn't care for *Pee-boon* either because a hard layer of water would form above him and there were no more flies or insects to feed on. *Kee-go* had to resort to his smaller brothers for food. Not only that but the strange white stuff that came from *Pee-boon's* breath would cover the hard layer and the water would get cold and dark. *Kee-go* would feel lazy and ceased to move around too much.

One day all the birds, animals, and fish met and discussed how they could keep *Pee-boon* from visiting them. "Why doesn't he stay where he comes from? Why does he have to come here?" they questioned. "Let's ask *Nana-boo-shoo*."

They all went to *Nana-boo-shoo* and asked him why *Pee-boon* came visiting and why he stayed so long. *Nana-boo-shoo* explained that were it not for *Pee-boon* all the trees, shrubs, and plants would soon die. When the leaves dry up and fall to Mother Earth they provide more food for the trees, bushes, and plants. *Nana-boo-shoo* explained that *Pee-boon* would never stay too long. When Brother Sun starts to get high in the northern sky *Pee-boon* leaves because he does not care for Brother Sun. Then one day soon after Mother Earth will welcome *Me-nou-kaw-me* (Spring) again.

Walk in Peace

NORTHERN LIGHTS AND WHY

Among the Indians of North America there are many beliefs which explain Mother Nature's wonders and why and how they happened. This is a story about Northern Lights.

The modern explanation is that the Aurora Borealis, or Northern Lights, which are seen only in the northern hemisphere, glow because of the presence of ionized particles in the atmosphere.

I remember seeing the lights for the first time as a young boy. I was amazed. The light red, pale green, blue and yellow-tinged lights moved and shifted in the sky; some spots were brighter than others. As I watched, the colors became more intense and seemed to move even faster. I asked my Mother what made them do that. She said, "I don't know."

But I knew who would–my Grandfather. When I told him what I had seen the night before and asked him what the lights meant he said, "People call them Northern Lights, but old Indians call them Spirit Lights and this is why."

When an Indian person goes on the Long Walk (dies), he goes through the Western door on his journey to the beyond. He takes his bow and arrows, his medicine bag, and plenty of food to last on this journey to the other world.

He visits his many friends who have gone before him. He meets his mother and father again in the "Big Village." There are many people from his youth. They are getting ready for the big Council meeting that night. They gather wood for the council fire, around which they will talk of many things and make decisions affecting their people.

Lighting the fire signified that the council meeting was going to begin. All the tribal chiefs were there. As each chief presented his problem or situation, the others advised and finally voted "for" or "against" it. The braves then danced around the fires.

The Northern Lights are these dancing braves. The sudden flashes of light that shoot up occur when more wood is thrown on the fire. The lights appear in the sky as long as the council is held and it will meet each night until all matters are settled to their liking.

This is the *A-nish-na-bee* (Indian People's) spiritual belief. Matters concerning the Mother Earth are settled by those who lived on it at one time. Meanwhile, the Great Spirit smiles on his people and guides them in their ways.

Walk in Peace

GLOSSARY

A-pung-ish-a-moog: Rains from west

Ah-jid-ah-moo: Red Squirrel

Au-dje-djawk: Crane

Au-ke-kaw-daw: Tamarack

Au-mick: Beaver

Au-pe-tchi: Robin

Au-saw-saw-go: Squirrel

Au-zhawshk: Muskrat

Aw-nib: Elm

Aw-shaw-way-nish: Beech tree

Awn-dayg: Crow

Chee-ma-gute: Skunk

Chi-wa-bik: Big Tooth

Chi-mon: Boat

Chingassanee: Big Sail

Da-bon: Car

Du-moo-ya-quay: Old Woman

Essikon: Raccoon

Ginebig: Snake

Giwedin: North (land)

Ga-wan-dag: Spruce

Inina-atig: Maple

Jo-bee: Muskrat (personal name)

Kagons: Porcupine

Kee-go: Fish

Kee-wa-zee: Old Man

Ke-zhek: Cedar

Kenui-ke-geshik: Bird That Flies at Night

Ke-way-di-noong: North wind

Manitou: Great Spirit, Great One, God

Maw-kwa: Bear

Maw-may: Sturgeon

Maw-maw-bin: Sucker

Maw-ne-ton: Insect, bug

May-may-gawn: Butterfly

Me-nou-kaw-me: Spring

Mino gijigad: It is a fine day.

Misko-bine-she: Cardinal

Mony-qua: Mary

Mo-say: Little worm

Mo-seh: Caterpillar, Wooly Bear

Muckwah-ne-bod: Sleeping Bear

Mujeekewis: West Wind

Mu-kaw-gee: Dog, a friend of the people

Nana-boo-shoo: A magician, trickster who can take on different forms for his advantage

Ne-bin: Summer

Nish-na-be: First Man

Nish-naw-bee: Indian people

Nish-na-bee-quay: First Woman

No-won-yaw: Air

O-doon-she-ke: Snapping turtle

Odawa: Ottawa

Ojibway: Chippewa

Omakoki: Frog

Ozaw-waw bine-shan: Canary

Paw-gaw-naw-ko-paw-gon: Black walnut

Pe-nay: Partridge

Pee-boon: Winter

Seeson: Susan

Shabo-e-guning: Cheyboygan

Shaw-wah-nong: South Wind

She-ke: Mud Turtle

She-sheb: Duck

Shin-gwawk: Pine

Tau-gwan-gee: Fall

Tchin-dee: Bluejay

Waboose: Rabbit

Wah-wah-tah-see: Firefly

We'we: Goose

Wing-ge-ze: Eagle

Wig-wasi: White Birch